PRODUCTIVITY THROUGH DATA SIMPLICITY

Your guide to data organization and standardization in Excel

Anthony Barbieri

2019

TABLE OF CONTENTS

Conclusion

About the Author

INTRODUCTION

Have you ever had to work with a spreadsheet where the data was so disorganized and inconsistent, it was practically unusable? Perhaps you needed to provide reports on a regular basis but had difficulty establishing a consistent and standardized process. Unfortunately, we have all had to deal with these types of issues before, which can make simple tasks dreadful to complete.

If you are interested in straightforward data organization and standardization techniques that will make your work easier and more efficient, then this book is for you!

GOAL OF THIS BOOK

I have seen some truly terrible Excel spreadsheets over the years – and I've decided it's time to help rid the world of disorganized data and clunky processes that complicate our work and waste time.

I am a business analytics (BA) professional working for an international consumer packaged goods company. A lot of my work is project-based and requires developing standardized reporting and analytical solutions for business users. I've used analytical tools such as Microsoft Power BI, SAP Web Intelligence, Qlikview, R, Python, and most commonly, Excel. All of these applications are fantastic and provide their own advantages when conducting analyses.

However, regardless of which project I work on or which tool I use, one thing is as certain as death and taxes: I always need to import and reference an Excel file! Whether it is an Excel file that contains sales data, customer information, or calendar mapping, an Excel file of some sort is always required.

No matter how hard I pray to the PivotTable gods, I cannot escape the atrocities committed in Excel spreadsheets. The disorganization, lack of consistency, and improper formatting (just to name a few), have become too much. I felt compelled to write a guide that will help people create organized, standardized, and more efficient spreadsheets for themselves and for those with whom they will be shared.

I want to rid the world of terrible spreadsheets so that we can focus more of our time analyzing data, instead of continuously fixing errors. Most importantly, I want to share my knowledge in a simple, clear way that can help anyone familiar with Excel understand these best practices, and help make their job less complicated. If you adopt the principles discussed in this book, I promise you will be well on your way to becoming your office's data superstar.

HOW THIS BOOK
IS ORGANIZED

In this book, I share data organization and standardization techniques as a series of principles. These principles will enable you to organize your data more efficiently in Excel, easily link your data to other sources, optimize your data for multiple purposes, and prevent unnecessary rework and wasted time. Some of these practices may seem obvious, but they are quite commonly violated.

The principles are broken out into two sections. The first section focuses on data organization. These principles are related to keeping the data in your Excel files clean, organized, and easy to use. The second section discusses data standardization principles. These principles will aid you in creating standardized processes that require little to no manual intervention. It is important to note that for the data standardization principles to be effective, the data organization principles must first be in place.

WHO THIS BOOK IS FOR

This book is meant for those who use or have used Excel or any other spreadsheet tool but are not familiar with data organization and standardization principles. It is meant for those who need to organize, standardize, or create reports in a spreadsheet on a regular basis.

While the principles discussed in this book are not technical in nature, it is recommended that you have had some experience using Excel (or other spreadsheet tools) and its commonly used formulas, in order to think about how you can apply the principles to your own data. This book will assume that you have a basic understanding of the commonly used formulas, as it will not provide detailed technical instruction on Excel functions.

DISCLAIMER

It is important to mention that this guide cannot cover every data organization and standardization principle out there. This book will discuss the principles that I commonly use (or wish others would use) throughout my career as a business analytics professional when handling Excel files.

I also acknowledge that there may be special cases when best practice principles may need to be suspended. I recognize that datasets may be unique and may have their own unique business rationale that prevents certain principles from being used. If this occurs, I encourage you to ask yourself if this logic can be changed, to ensure data is organized and processes are standardized more efficiently.

Some of the principles mentioned in this book (primarily the ones in the Data Organization section) stem from database design rules, known as Rules of Normalization, and are grounded in best practices recognized by universities and technology companies such as Microsoft. If you are curious, you can visit the Microsoft website that discusses the basics of database normalization here: https://support.microsoft.com/en-ca/help/283878/description-of-the-database-normalization-basics

COPYRIGHT

Anthony Barbieri

technological measures that legally restrict others from doing anything the license permits.

To view the Legal Code, please visit:
https://creativecommons.org/licenses/by-sa/4.0/legalcode

PART I: DATA ORGANIZATION PRINCIPLES

This section will outline principles you should follow when organizing data in Excel. It discusses how to format and organize your data so that you can become more efficient, spend less time modifying your data and more time on your analysis. These principles will also enable you to use the data in your spreadsheet for additional purposes in the future.

PRINCIPLE #1: FORMAT YOUR DATA IN A TABLE

I might be stating the obvious here, but I'll say it anyway: *always organize your data in a **table** format.* Excel was designed to house structured data. Your raw data should always be placed within rows and columns, and columns should always be named (*Figure 1.1*). The table in *Figure 1.1* shows how data should be organized. It is easy to tell which pieces of data are Products, Customers, and Sales.

Columns		
Product	Customer	Sale
A	X	100
B	Y	50
C	Z	200

Figure 1.1: Data properly organized in a table format

You should never have data floating around in different parts of your spreadsheet or in random cells (*Figure 1.2*).

			C	Z	200
A	X	100			
B	Y	50			

Figure 1.2: Data improperly organized

It is impossible to know what the data in *Figure 1.2* represents. If the data was shared with a colleague, you would need to clarify what it represents, and format the data so that it looks similar to the table in *Figure 1.1*. This causes unnecessary confusion and wasted time.

Organizing your data in a table format with named columns will help you and others understand it more easily and create Excel formulas that reference the data without any required cleansing or formatting. For example, it is easy to calculate the total number of sales in *Figure 1.1* by using a simple SUM function that references all the cells in the Sale column. Achieving a sum with the data in *Figure 1.2* is still possible, but requires a customized formula that manually references the 200 value.

PRINCIPLE #2: ADD EXTRA COLUMNS IF NEEDED

If you find your data is too ambiguous and lacks detail, don't be afraid to add more columns to your table. Additional columns give you the opportunity to add more characteristics to your data, giving it more detail and depth.

For example, building upon the table in *Figure 1.1* from Principle #1, you may want to know *where* each sale took place. For some people, their immediate instinct is to create several different tables for each region. If this was your initial instinct, I suggest you take a break to splash some cold water on your face and come back when that idea is long gone.

The best approach to a situation like this is to add a column for Region or State (*Figure 2.1*). Once it has been added, it will look something like this:

Product	Customer	State	Sale
A	X	New York	100
B	Y	New York	50
C	Z	Nevada	200

Figure 2.1: State column added to table

You can add as many columns as needed in order to get the

level of detail required (*Figure 2.2*):

Product	Customer	State	Rep	Sale	Units
A	X	New York	Sally	100	5
B	Y	New York	Sally	50	10
C	Z	Nevada	Steve	200	50

Figure 2.2: Rep and Units columns added to table

Adding columns when needed allows you to keep your data in one organized table while providing detail and depth. With this approach, you can apply filters to any column and restrict your data selection(s) as you wish. You are also able to apply SUMIF or COUNTIF formulas (to name a few) that reference and calculate the columns needed, which would not be so easy to do if you had created 50 different tables for every state!

PRINCIPLE #3: CELLS MUST NOT CONTAIN MULTIPLE VALUES

This principle is near and dear to my heart, as I have encountered this issue an endless amount of times. Each of the cells within a column should only contain **one** value. For example, if you have a column named "State", each of the cells should only contain one state name (i.e. "New York", or "Missouri", etc.). In this example, you should never place "New York, Missouri" in the same cell.

Figure 3.1 provides a clear example of what you should <u>not</u> do:

Product	Customer	State	Sale ($)
A	X	New York, Missouri	100
B	Y	New York, Missouri	50
C	Z	Nevada, California	200

Figure 3.1: Example of multiple values in a cell

There are a few issues with the setup in *Figure 3.1*. The first issue is the uncertainly of whether a sale of $100 for Product A and Customer X occurred for New York <u>and</u> Missouri (independently), actually resulting in a $200 sale, or whether the $100 sale is a cumulative total for <u>both</u> states. Unfortunately, you won't be able to know without asking the person who made the spreadsheet.

The second issue with the setup in *Figure 3.1* is that it would prevent you from performing a sales analysis by state. For example, what if you wanted to use a SUMIF formula that tells you the total sales for Product A that occurred in New York only? With the current setup, you won't be able to easily find that answer by doing a simple SUMIF. You would need to perform some formula acrobatics to resolve it.

Now, I'm sure you Excel whizzes reading this right now believe you can easily write a formula to find the answer. I have no doubt that you can, but that assumes that the sales dollars listed actually occurred within each state, and is not a cumulative total. If it is cumulative, then there is no formula that will help you.

So, how do we solve this issue? We would need to break out the sale(s) that occurred within each state by adding rows.

Figure 3.2 provides a clear example of what you should do:

Product	Customer	State	Sale ($)
A	X	New York	80
A	X	Missouri	20
B	Y	New York	15
B	Y	Missouri	35
C	Z	Nevada	50
C	Z	Nevada	150

Figure 3.2: Example of cells that do not contain multiple values

As you can see in the table above, this way you can easily tell which sales took place in each state without second-guessing yourself, or having to ask the author of the spreadsheet as to whether the sales are cumulative or not. You are also able to create simple formulas (i.e. SUMIF) that can tell you the total sales for a particular product or bought by a particular customer by state.

As a general tip, if you need to perform formula acrobatics to find an answer that should have been resolved with a simple formula, than there is a good chance that the data you are using is organized incorrectly.

PRINCIPLE #4: COLUMNS MUST ONLY CONTAIN DATA OF THE SAME TYPE

You should not mix different data types (i.e. customer name, address, city, etc.) in the same column. For example, if you have a column named "Customer Name", you must only place customer names within that column (*Figure 4.1*). You should *never* place things like city names, state names, or anything else in that column. This principle may seem obvious, but it is surprising to see how often it is violated.

Figure 4.1 shows an example of this principle being violated:

Customer Name	Address	City	State
Dylan's Diner	12 Sunnyside Lane	San Francisco	California
Sally's Supermarket	34 Brightlights Dr	Nevada	Las Vegas
Bobby's Bread Basket	56 Yeast Blvd	Seattle	Washington
78 Grill Road	Carla's Cookhouse	Phoenix	Arizona

Figure 4.1: Shows columns containing different data types

With this current setup, you are ultimately creating unreliable data (also known as "garbage data") that would be difficult or impossible for anyone to use for analytical or reporting purposes. Someone would need to go through all of the raw data and manually correct all of the incorrect cells. Worse yet – imagine you needed to receive this disorganized data from someone on a regular basis in order to perform tasks at work. You would either need to manually correct the data every time you receive a new file (which may not be practical if the file contained thousands of rows), write complex or unnecessary formulas that handle every exception, or you can decide that you've had enough of this madness and join the circus! Fortunately, there is a much better option, and that is to just never place different data types in the same column.

To solve this issue is simple: just place each data type within its respective column. See *Figure 4.2* for an example:

Customer Name	Address	City	State
Dylan's Diner	12 Sunnyside Lane	San Francisco	California
Sally's Supermarket	34 Brightlights Dr	Las Vegas	Nevada
Bobby's Bread Basket	56 Yeast Blvd	Seattle	Washington
Carla's Cookhouse	78 Grill Road	Phoenix	Arizona

Figure 4.2: Shows columns containing one data type

Ah, much better!

PRINCIPLE #5: COLUMN NAMES SHOULD BE UNIQUE

Every column you create in your spreadsheets should always have a unique name. Your column names should never be duplicated or given a similar name to a column that already exists. For example, if you have a spreadsheet that is tracking inventory from multiple suppliers and have a column for Supplier Name, you should not have several columns named Supplier Name or any variation, as depicted in *Figure 5.1* below.

Country	Inventory Units		
	Supplier 1	Supplier 2	Supplier 3
Canada	100	60	150
United States	20	200	10
France	50	100	70
Japan	80	10	100

Figure 5.1: Column names are not unique

You might wonder, "what's wrong with the table in *Figure 5.1*?" Indeed, there may be times when you might be requested to present data in this format. There is no problem creating *reports* in this format, but the problem occurs when you store your *raw data* this way. Raw data should never be stored in this format.

Storing your raw data using similar column names will require you to create formulas that are static and can only be applied to one supplier. This might not be an issue if you only have a few suppliers, or perhaps only a few products in your data. But what happens if you get a new supplier, or manufacture a new product? You will now need to go back to your spreadsheets (you know you'll need to edit more than one) and create or adjust your formulas to accommodate the new supplier or product columns.

Having only a few suppliers or products is unrealistic. You will most likely have several or dozens of suppliers and hundreds of products. Do you plan to go back to every spreadsheet and add each new product or supplier as a new column, resulting in an unwieldly document? Would you rather waste your time fiddling with formula references instead of *analyzing* your data? If you answered "yes" to any of these questions, then I place my hands over my face and shake my head from side-to-side.

For those who seek to be more efficient in their data organization, have no fear – there is a way around this issue. *Figure 5.2* shows the principle in action:

Country	Supplier #	Inventory Units
Canada	1	100
Canada	2	60
Canada	3	150
United States	1	20
United States	2	200
United States	3	10
France	1	50
France	2	100
France	3	70
Japan	1	80
Japan	2	10
Japan	3	100

Figure 5.2: Column names are unique

All of the columns in the updated table are now unique. With this setup, you are able to add or remove as many suppliers and inventory units as you like without impacting your formulas, since the formulas will always reference the same columns every time. You are also able to easily create PivotTables and update them in the format of your choice when new data is added – something you couldn't do in *Figure 5.1*.

Raw data should always be organized and clean. You should never treat your raw data as a report. As a simple guide, well-organized raw data generally does not look visually pleasing. If it does, you most likely did something wrong. A table structure with rows and columns may not be attractive, but it is clean and functional. Instead, let your creative juices flow when it comes to designing end-user reports. These reports will reference your raw data. If your raw data is well organized, you will have any easier and faster time modifying your reports' format to meet the needs of your organization.

PRINCIPLE #6: SPELL VALUES CONSISTENTLY

This is probably one of the easiest principles to follow, but it is often the most violated. This principle simply states that no matter what value you enter into your cells, always ensure that they are spelled consistently – every time.

For example, if you have a Country column in your table and one of the countries is the United States, always ensure that you spell "United States" consistently – whether that involves spelling it "United States", "United States of America", or "USA". No matter what you choose, ensure that you spell it the same way every time.

If you don't spell your values consistently, you'll end up with a table that looks like this (*Figure 6.1*):

Supplier	Source Country	Inventory Units
Supplier 1	Canada	100
Supplier 2	United States	60
Supplier 3	France	150
Supplier 4	Japan	20
Supplier 5	Canada	200
Supplier 6	US	10
Supplier 7	France	50
Supplier 8	Japan	100
Supplier 9	Canada	70
Supplier 10	USA	80
Supplier 11	France	10
Supplier 12	Japan	100

Figure 6.1: Values are not spelled consistently

The problem with inconsistent values in your data is that it makes it difficult to apply filters and write formulas. If you wanted to write a formula that calculated the sum of all inventory units for the United States, you would need to tell the formula to find values in the Source Country column that are equal to "United States", "US", and "USA". Quite annoying, isn't it? And that is just *one* country! Image if you had to do the same for other countries?

Now, it may not be so bad if your dataset is small, since you can quickly find the inconsistent values and replace them. However, having a small dataset in the real world is unlikely, and constantly changing dozens of values in your data is time consuming, cumbersome, and ultimately unnecessary.

To ensure there are no misunderstandings, here is what consistent values in a table look like (*Figure 6.2*):

Supplier	Source Country	Inventory Units
Supplier 1	Canada	100
Supplier 2	United States	60
Supplier 3	France	150
Supplier 4	Japan	20
Supplier 5	Canada	200
Supplier 6	United States	10
Supplier 7	France	50
Supplier 8	Japan	100
Supplier 9	Canada	70
Supplier 10	United States	80
Supplier 11	France	10
Supplier 12	Japan	100

Figure 6.2: Values are spelled consistently

Based on my experience, inconsistent values are primarily caused by one of two things: 1) There is more than one person inputting data into the same spreadsheet, or 2) The sole person inputting the data is (mentally) out to lunch. If you are collaborating with others, ensure that you agree on a standardized list of values to input beforehand. If you rely on spreadsheets that are authored by someone who is inconsistent in their data input, try talking to them and teach them the importance and benefits of entering values consistently.

PRINCIPLE #7: USE KEYS WHEN POSSIBLE

It is always ideal to associate your data to an ID or key. A key is a unique value that is associated to a row or cell value. If you need to find certain values or records, it is much easier to reference on a key than a cell containing text.

For example, let's take a look at the table in *Figure 7.1*:

Product Name Desc	Sales ($)
Blue Jeans Comfort Fit Size S	100
Blue Jeans Comfort Fit Size M	200
Blue Jeans Comfort Fit Size L	150
Black Jeans Comfort Fit Size S	100
Black Jeans Comfort Fit Size M	100
Black Jeans Comfort Fit Size L	80
Dress Shirt White Size S	70
Dress Shirt White Size M	60
Dress Shirt White Size L	50

Figure 7.1: Product Name Description
column without associated keys

The table above shows a list of clothes products with an associated sale value. When you don't have an associated key column, in this case for Product Name Desc, you solely rely on the accuracy and consistency of the product name description to identify the products. This may not be a problem if you spell the product description *exactly* the same, without typos or extra spaces, every time.

The table above *(Figure 7.1)* shows a column with product names spelled consistently and ultimately created in a vacuum. As you may know, these types of tables rarely exist in the real world. Instead, they look similar to what is shown in *Figure 7.2*:

Product Name Desc	Units Sold
Blue Jeans Comf Fit Sz S	25
BJcomfortfitsizem	30
Blue J Com Fit Size Large	55
Black Jean Comfort Fit Size Small	90
Black Jeans Comfort Fit Size M	10
BLK Jean comf size large	40
dress shirt white s	60
Shirt M	85
Size L White Dress Shirt	70

Figure 7.2: Product Name Description column with in-consistent spelling and no associated keys

That looks a bit more realistic, doesn't it? Now, what if you wanted to associate or link the Sales ($) column from *Figures 7.1* to the Units Sold column in *Figures 7.2*? With the names inconsistently spelled in *Figure 7.2*, it would be extremely difficult to do. Luckily, there is a better way – with keys!

Figure 7.3 shows the Product Name Desc column from both tables being associated to a Product ID or key:

Product ID	Product Name Desc	Sales ($)
1231	Blue Jeans Comfort Fit Size S	100
1232	Blue Jeans Comfort Fit Size M	200
1233	Blue Jeans Comfort Fit Size L	150
1234	Black Jeans Comfort Fit Size S	100
1235	Black Jeans Comfort Fit Size M	100
1236	Black Jeans Comfort Fit Size L	80
1237	Dress Shirt White Size S	70
1238	Dress Shirt White Size M	60
1239	Dress Shirt White Size L	50

Product ID	Product Name Desc	Units Sold
1231	Blue Jeans Comf Fit Sz S	25
1232	BJcomfortfitsizem	30
1233	Blue J Com Fit Size Large	55
1234	Black Jean Comfort Fit Size Small	90
1235	Black Jeans Comfort Fit Size M	10
1236	BLK Jean comf size large	40
1237	dress shirt white s	60
1238	Shirt M	85
1239	Size L White Dress Shirt	70

Figure 7.3: Sales ($) and Units Sold tables now have a Product ID, allowing the products to be easily identifiable

With both tables now containing a Product ID, you are able to easily reference or VLOOKUP the product keys from either table and find the Sales ($) and Units Sold amounts for each product.

Keys make your life so much easier. While not all columns will have a corresponding key, if they do, you should most definitely always use them.

PRINCIPLE #8: FORMAT DATES THE "RIGHT" WAY

This is a principle that I cannot emphasize enough. There is one way, and one way only, in which you should format your date values, especially if you plan on referencing them to another date column in another table. That format is as follows: **YYYYMMDD**.

I'm not the only one who feels strongly about date formats. The International Organization of Standardization (ISO) also recommends that dates should be written as YYYYMMDD. Their standard, ISO 8601, supports this format. You can take a look for yourself here: https://www.iso.org/iso-8601-date-and-time-format.html

To break it down: *YYYY* stands for the year (e.g. 2019), *MM* stands for the month (e.g. 04), and *DD* stands for day (e.g. 16). For example, let's say I wanted to format July 28, 2018. This date, formatted as "YYYYMMDD", would look like: 20180728.

There are a few benefits to formatting your dates this way.

First, this date format is consistent and follows a logical descending order from *year* to *month* to *day*, similar to an actual calendar. There is no need for confusion or to second guess the order of a date if it follows the YYYYMMDD format. Let's take this date for example: 06-05-2019. It is difficult to know if the "06" or the "05" represents the month or the day. However, using the YY-YYMMDD format prevents this confusion and uncertainty from occurring. The consistency of the YYYYMMDD format makes it easy to use the LEFT, MID, and RIGHT functions to extract parts of the date. For example, it is simple to extract the Year, Month, and Day values and store them in their own columns (*Figure 8.1*).

YYYYMMDD	Year	Month	Day
20190101	2019	01	01
20190102	2019	01	02
20190203	2019	02	03
20190204	2019	02	04
20190305	2019	03	05
20190306	2019	03	06
20190407	2019	04	07
20190408	2019	04	08
20190509	2019	05	09

Figure 8.1: Date attributes are extracted from the YYYYMMDD column

Second, sorting your data by date is extremely easy in the YY-YYMMDD format. It is also easy to find a date you are looking for. As mentioned, this format follows a logical descending order. So if you need to sort your data in descending or ascending order, your data will be grouped logically, first by year, followed by month, and then day (*Figure 8.2*).

YYYYMMDD	Date Desc
20190101	January 1, 2019
20190102	January 2, 2019
20190203	February 3, 2019
20190204	February 4, 2019
20190305	March 5, 2019
20190306	March 6, 2019
20190407	April 7, 2019
20190408	April 8, 2019
20190509	May 9, 2019

Figure 8.2: Date column (YYYYMMDD) is sorted in ascending order

Third, the YYYYMMDD format allows you to easily reference /

VLOOKUP other calendar attributes from another spreadsheet if needed. Simply put, the YYYYMMDD values make an excellent key, as per Principle #7. Since the YYYYMMDD format does not contain any slashes or dashes (e.g. 2018-07-28), you can convert the values to either a number or to a text data type, depending on the date format in the other spreadsheet. Of course, this only works if the other spreadsheet has a YYYYMMDD column as well. If not, the dates in the other spreadsheet will need to be reformatted so that it can properly reference your YYYYMMDD column.

To be clear, YYYYMMDD does not need to be the one and only date column in your spreadsheets. You are free to have as many date columns as you wish, formatted any way you like, as long as you include *one* date column that is formatted as YYYYMMDD. Having this particular date column not only provides you with the benefits mentioned above, but it will also save you time, effort, and mental anguish.

PRINCIPLE #9: AVOID PARTIAL DEPENDENCIES

This principle may be more commonly used with databases, as opposed to Excel spreadsheets, since partial dependencies take up extra storage space. However, the same benefits apply.

This principle states that your table should not contain columns that rely on multiple key/ID columns. This reliance is known as a partial dependency. While partial dependencies are not a serious faux-pas, they should be avoided since they require you to maintain multiple sets of data in the same table, update multiple cells related to a key column if a data change occurs, and take up unnecessary space and storage.

Take a look at *Figure 9.1* for an example:

A	B	C	D	E	F	G
Customer ID	Customer Name	Customer State	Product ID	Product Name	Pack Size	Sale ($)
123	ABC	California	159874	Beverage 1	12x8oz	5,000
123	ABC	California	156320	Beverage 2	6x6oz	3,000
789	GHI	New York	159874	Beverage 1	12x8oz	9,000
789	GHI	New York	235689	Beverage 3	24x8oz	500
654	MNO	New York	241025	Beverage 4	12x3oz	450
753	PQR	Missouri	156320	Beverage 2	6x6oz	2,000
951	STU	California	510236	Beverage 5	12x8oz	2,700
201	VWX	Arizona	456019	Beverage 6	24x8oz	6,000
380	YZZ	Texas	235689	Beverage 3	24x8oz	1,000

Figure 9.1: Partial dependency columns (orange) rely on multiple ID columns (purple)

Columns **A** and **D** in the table above are Customer and Product IDs. Columns **B** and **C** are customer attributes and are dependent on Column **A**, while Columns **E** and **F** are product attributes and are dependent on Column **D**. To avoid creating partial dependencies, the dependent columns (i.e. **B**, **C**, **E**, and **F**) should be removed from the table.

So what would that look like? It would require creating two additional tables, one for Customer and one for Product, and removing columns **B**, **C**, **E**, and **F** from *Figure 9.1*. The redesign of *Figure 9.1* can be seen in *Figure 9.2*. This would be your main table, and the two new tables, seen in *Figure 9.2.1* and *9.2.2*, would be your new attribute tables.

Customer ID	Product ID	Sale ($)
123	159874	5,000
123	156320	3,000
789	159874	9,000
789	235689	500
654	241025	450
753	156320	2,000
951	510236	2,700
201	456019	6,000
380	235689	1,000

Figure 9.2: New "main" table. Partial dependency columns have been removed.

Customer ID	Customer Name	Customer State
123	ABC	California
201	VWX	Arizona
380	YZZ	Texas
654	MNO	New York
753	PQR	Missouri
789	GHI	New York
951	STU	California

Figure 9.2.1: Newly created Customer table. Contains unique rows.

Product ID	Product Name	Pack Size
156320	Beverage 2	6x6oz
159874	Beverage 1	12x8oz
235689	Beverage 3	24x8oz
241025	Beverage 4	12x3oz
456019	Beverage 6	24x8oz
510236	Beverage 5	12x8oz

Figure 9.2.2: Newly created Product table. Contains unique rows.

We are able to store all the Customer and Product attributes in the two newly created tables, while keeping our main table (*Figure 9.2*) free from partial dependencies. This allows us to maintain unique Customer and Product information in one location. That means, if a product or customer name change occurs, we would only need to update the Customer and Product tables. Since each row in both of these tables is unique, we would only need to update the information once, instead of the old setup from *Figure 9.1*, which would require updating duplicated values in multiple cells.

I realize that this setup may not always be feasible and that you may require the partial dependencies and attributes to be part of one table in certain situations. But before you dismiss this principle, try this first: simply create VLOOKUP formulas that reference the ID columns (in this case Product ID and Customer ID from *Figure 9.2*) and lookup the related attributes (Customer Name, Product Name, etc.) from *Figure 9.2.1* and *9.2.2*. This way, if a change is made to the Customer or Product tables (*Figures 9.2.1* and *9.2.2*), it will be reflected automatically within your main table (*Figure 9.2*). Who doesn't want automation?

PART II: DATA STANDARDIZATION PRINCIPLES

The principles in this section are geared towards those who regularly use or update spreadsheets that need to be inputted into other Excel files or business analytics tools for reporting purposes. In addition to building on the principles in the Data Organization section, this section will outline principles that will help you successfully implement automatic or semi-automatic solutions (depending on whether you are using a special business analytics tool or only Excel) that require the use of one or more Excel files.

PRINCIPLE #10: ALWAYS KNOW YOUR DATA

There are many times when people eagerly (and blindly) jump into a data project without fully understanding the data. They have no idea how their data sources are going to connect, the commonalities between the sources, or whether the data is even usable! As such, this principle states that you must always get to know your data before using it.

Knowing your data is important because it allows you to analyze or walkthrough your data in order to understand the different columns being used, the cleanliness and usability of the data itself (including adherence to the principles discussed in this book) and how it links to other sources, if any.

It may seem intuitive that anyone working with any dataset would first come to understand the data, and how they are or are not related. However, it is not unlikely for this principle to be ignored, especially if those working with the datasets lack proper data experience or are given a task from their managers that must be completed quickly. Preventing the former from occurring is simple, since you can educate yourself on data organization and standardization principles (such as reading this book!).

Being given a task that must be completed quickly, especially by a superior, is a trickier situation to handle. While it may be difficult, my recommendation is for you to immediately let your manager or project stakeholders know that the data you have been asked to use is dirty or may not be linkable to other sources (i.e. lacks a common key column). You can also try suggesting recommendations to resolve the issue, such as requesting the same data from somewhere else, or asking the owner of this data to clean it up before use.

The point here is, if you do not get to know your data early on, quality or usability issues may only surface when it is difficult to address them. You should always know what you are dealing with and how your datasets connect to one another at the project outset – otherwise you'll be completing your project as if you're walking through a construction site in the fog. Quite a dangerous place to be.

PRINCIPLE #11:
KEEP YOUR NAMING CONVENTIONS STATIC AND CONSISTENT

When it comes to standardization and/or automation, it is essential that your file names, tab names, and column names remain static – unchanged—and that you stick to consistent naming conventions as established within your process. This is necessary if you plan to use an Excel file as a data source for other Excel files, or input it into a business analytics tool (i.e. Power BI, Qlikview, Tableau, etc.).

Keeping the filename, tab names, and column names static will allow your process to run successfully and prevent any "breakage" and manual maintenance. If your Excel report or BA tool is referencing a particular file, tab, and column(s), and you decide to change any of the names, then there is a very high chance that your process will go off the rails.

This principle is likely to be violated when your process relies on someone else's Excel files. Those files may not have originally been intended to be used for your report/process, so the owner(s) may change the filename, tab names, or column names at any time.

In order to prevent this issue, you can try the following:

1) If you own/maintain the Excel data files that will feed into your process/report, *don't make any changes to the naming conventions!* That is easy enough.

2) If your data sources are owned or maintained by someone else, see if they can keep the naming convention the same at all times.

3) While not as automatic as you may like, if you don't own or maintain the Excel data files and you know the filename, tab names, and/or column names are guaranteed to change, you can copy and paste the data from the data source into your own Excel template file, where you have complete control over the naming conventions. More on this in Principle #16.

PRINCIPLE #12: NEW COLUMNS BELONG ON THE RIGHT

While the names of columns should remain static and never change (as discussed in Principle #11), they should also always remain in the same position. When establishing a standardized and/or automated process, the column positions (as well as their names) should not be changed. If a process has already been established, an Excel file(s) is already being referenced, and a new column needs to be added, the new column should be placed on the *far right side of the table*.

For example, let's take a look at *Figure 12.1*:

Country	Region	City
Australia	New South Wales	Sydney
Brazil	Center-West	Brasilia
Canada	Ontario	Toronto
Iceland	Capital Region	Reykjavík
India	Maharashtra	Mumbai
Italy	Lazio	Rome
New Zealand	Canterbury	Christchurch
South Africa	Western Cape	Cape Town
United States	Nevada	Las Vegas

Figure 12.1: Table showing country, region, and city

Let's assume that *Figure 12.1* is our original table and feeds into a report that is part of a standardized process. Now let's assume a new requirement is raised after our reporting process has been established, which requires the continent name to be added. Based on our understanding of this principle, where should the new column go?

That's right – on the far-right side of the table. For an example, *Figure 12.2* shows the updated table with the newly added column at the *far right*:

Country	Region	City	Continent
Australia	New South Wales	Sydney	Oceania
Brazil	Center-West	Brasilia	South America
Canada	Ontario	Toronto	North America
Iceland	Capital Region	Reykjavík	Europe
India	Maharashtra	Mumbai	Asia
Italy	Lazio	Rome	Europe
New Zealand	Canterbury	Christchurch	Oceania
South Africa	Western Cape	Cape Town	Africa
United States	Nevada	Las Vegas	North America

Figure 12.2: Table with newly added "Continent" column

Placing new columns in between existing columns may interfere with VLOOKUP formulas and other existing references, causing the formulas to reference the wrong columns. This is because Excel formulas such as VLOOKUPs reference a column based on its *position*, not its name. In contrast, if you are using a business analytics application, it may be referencing the column by its *name* instead of its position. Each application is different and you would need to know the traits of the one you are using. To ensure that your references/formulas are not affected by the addition of new columns, it is safest to always place them on the far right side of the table.

PRINCIPLE #13: DATA SHOULD RESIDE IN ONE TAB

There have been too many times when I have seen (and had to deal with) raw data broken out into multiple Excel tabs. Each tab contained similar data and was given its own name, usually to reflect a different time period or product groupings (i.e. Category A sales, Category B sales, Category C sales, etc.). While it may at times seem logical to group data into multiple tabs, you should avoid doing so. Instead, all data should reside within **one** tab – nothing more.

Breaking out data into multiple tabs creates complexity and increased effort when it comes time to analyze your data and write formulas. It also prevents you from conducting proper analyses, as you can only analyze the data within its own tab, making it difficult to conduct cross-analyses between tabs.

Figure 13.1 and *Figure 13.2* provides an example:

Year	Month	Continent	Category	Product	Customer
2019	Jan	Africa	Category A	Product 1	Customer 1
2019	Jan	Asia	Category A	Product 1	Customer 2
2019	Feb	Europe	Category A	Product 1	Customer 3
2019	Feb	Europe	Category A	Product 2	Customer 3
2018	Mar	North America	Category A	Product 2	Customer 4
2018	Apr	North America	Category A	Product 3	Customer 4
2018	May	Oceania	Category A	Product 4	Customer 5
2018	Jun	Oceania	Category A	Product 4	Customer 6
2018	Jun	South America	Category A	Product 4	Customer 7

Figure 13.1: Table in the "Category A" tab

Year	Month	Continent	Category	Product	Customer
2019	Jan	Africa	Category B	Product 12	Customer 1
2019	Jan	Asia	Category B	Product 14	Customer 2
2019	Feb	Europe	Category B	Product 16	Customer 3
2019	Feb	Europe	Category B	Product 21	Customer 3
2018	Mar	North America	Category B	Product 28	Customer 4
2018	Apr	North America	Category B	Product 30	Customer 4
2018	May	Oceania	Category B	Product 41	Customer 5
2018	Jun	Oceania	Category B	Product 41	Customer 6
2018	Jun	South America	Category B	Product 50	Customer 7

Figure 13.2: Table in the "Category B" tab

In these figures, you can see the sales data for Category A and Category B. If I asked you to tell me which customers purchased products from Category A, would you have any difficulties doing so? You wouldn't, since your data is organized by categories.

However, in this configuration you can only answer business questions that are specific to a single category. You are not able to conduct cross-analyses between the product categories.
For example, would you be able to tell which customer bought the most product from *any* category in the table above? Which year, month, or region had the most sales from *any* category? Are there any customers buying multiple products at the same time from *any* category? If so, which ones? The questions are endless. However, you can only answer them easily when your raw data is organized within one single tab (*Figure 13.3*), allowing for cross-category analysis.

Year	Month	Continent	Category	Product	Customer
2019	Jan	Africa	Category A	Product 1	Customer 1
2019	Jan	Asia	Category A	Product 1	Customer 2
2019	Feb	Europe	Category A	Product 1	Customer 3
2019	Feb	Europe	Category A	Product 2	Customer 3
2018	Mar	North America	Category A	Product 2	Customer 4
2018	Apr	North America	Category A	Product 3	Customer 4
2018	May	Oceania	Category A	Product 4	Customer 5
2018	Jun	Oceania	Category A	Product 4	Customer 6
2018	Jun	South America	Category A	Product 4	Customer 7
2019	Jan	Africa	Category B	Product 12	Customer 1
2019	Jan	Asia	Category B	Product 14	Customer 2
2019	Feb	Europe	Category B	Product 16	Customer 3
2019	Feb	Europe	Category B	Product 21	Customer 3
2018	Mar	North America	Category B	Product 28	Customer 4
2018	Apr	North America	Category B	Product 30	Customer 4
2018	May	Oceania	Category B	Product 41	Customer 5
2018	Jun	Oceania	Category B	Product 41	Customer 6
2018	Jun	South America	Category B	Product 50	Customer 7

Figure 13.3: Data is organized into one tab

Having your data in one tab allows you to conduct in-depth analyses, and increases your chances of discovering insights that will help your organization.

PRINCIPLE #14: FILE AND LOCATION PATHS MUST BE STATIC

Similar to what was discussed in Principle #11, you should ensure that your Excel file names and folder locations do not change and remain static. This is important when establishing a standardized process. If your file names and file locations keep changing, you would need to constantly update your process and reference the correct file and location.

You need to put some thought into your file name and ensure that it encapsulates what the file contains, without making references to changing pieces of information. For example, having a filename such as "Sales 2019" is not ideal if you plan to include sales data that goes beyond 2019. Likewise, naming a file "Product X sales" if you foresee the file containing sales information for other products would be problematic. In cases like this, foresight is key. Anticipate that more data will be added to the file and name the file based on what the data *represents,* rather than the values it contains (i.e. "Customer sales" instead of "Sales 2019", and "Product sales" instead of "Product X sales").

You will also need to consider where your Excel files should be stored. This is important if you are running a regular process that references files in other locations. Similar to the filenames, if file locations or folder names keep changing, you will need to constantly update your file's references in order for your formulas and processes to work. Again, apply some foresight and think about the file folder location. Is the file saved where the owner can access it? Is the file stored within a series of many sub-folders where it shouldn't be? Perhaps the folder name references an outdated year and needs to be changed to something that can remain static and consistent. Changes such as these will impact the reliability of your process, requiring continuous maintenance and wasted time – and who has time for that?

PRINCIPLE #15: CUSTOMIZATION IS YOUR ENEMY!

Let's face facts: customization is often unavoidable. However, be very cautious if you are required to do *a lot* of it. It can spin out of control very quickly.

I define customization as having to alter, regroup, or correct any of the raw data you are using in your reports, typically requiring formulas or scripts. Customization tends to occur because there is an issue or disconnect in the process that requires a correction in the original dataset. For example, if an original dataset's customer hierarchy is grouped a certain way, and you are required to adjust this grouping another way, then there is a disconnect between what the customer groupings are and what they should be. Instead of having to perform this manual adjustment, the hierarchy should be corrected in the original dataset.

Figure 15.1.1 shows an example of an outdated customer hierarchy present in the original dataset, and *Figure 15.1.2* shows the updated customer hierarchy as requested by business users:

Customer Group	Customer ID	Customer Name
A	123	Cust. 1
D	456	Cust. 2
C	789	Cust. 3
C	234	Cust. 4
A	567	Cust. 5
B	890	Cust. 6
B	345	Cust. 7

Figure 15.1.1: Example of an <u>outdated</u> customer hierarchy present in the original dataset

Customer Group	Customer ID	Customer Name
A	123	Cust. 1
A	456	Cust. 2
B	789	Cust. 3
C	234	Cust. 4
D	567	Cust. 5
D	890	Cust. 6
D	345	Cust. 7

Figure 15.1.2: Example of an <u>updated</u> customer hierarchy as requested by business users

Another example of customization is when invalid sales data is present in a dataset and needs to be excluded from end-user reports. It may be feasible to exclude *known* incorrect values that appear continuously in a dataset, but it is best that these issues get resolved in the original data source. It is also rare that all *known* errors are found and filtered out, especially if new errors are likely to occur. It is difficult and labour-intensive to keep track of these types of issues and continuously adjust your reports' formula logic.

It is always best that any modifications to the dataset, whether it is related to hierarchies or incorrect values, be corrected in the *original* dataset, and not within the reporting application. Ignoring this principle will ultimately cause complexity and numerous hours of continued maintenance.

If customization does need to occur, particularly with reclassification, it should be done using data keys, and not text values. For example, if you need to reassign certain products into another category, your formulas should use product codes (e.g. 45689345) and category codes (e.g. CAT0123) instead of product names (e.g. "Bluetooth headset with microphone") or category names (e.g. "Audio communication devices").

As mentioned, some customization will inevitably be required when creating reports. However, you must use your judgement and decide whether the requested customization is necessary and sustainable. Customization should only occur if the data alteration or correction can be done using *static* formulas or logic that does not need to be changed in the future. You should never need to continuously update your customized formulas or groupings on a monthly, weekly, or daily basis in order to accommodate new and changing data. This is what nightmares are made of!

If you are forced to implement customized formulas or logic that you know are not sustainable and will require continuous maintenance and wasted time, speak to the requestor or project team and explain why the requests are not recommended. If your advice is dismissed, document and log the pros (if any) and cons of the requests, state your recommendation and the team's official agreed-upon direction, and communicate it to the project team/stakeholders. You will need this documentation when you are asked why the report you have created is not sustainable and requires continuous maintenance.

PRINCIPLE #16: ORGANIZE DATA IN PHASES

If you need to regularly update or insert raw data into your Excel reports, it is best that you organize your data in phases. This will allow you to have a dedicated "landing" tab for your raw data, while having another tab to perform any data modifications such as changes to format or order of the data structure, create formulas or new columns, etc. This principle goes hand-in-hand with Principle #13, since it can only work if all of your raw data is consolidated and inputted into one tab.

Organizing your data in phases gives you more control over your data. To explain how you would organize your data in phases, your Excel file may contain the following tabs as shown in *Figure 16.1*:

| Input | Staging | Report |

Figure 16.1: Example of tabs used in an Excel file
to organize data in phases

The **input** tab (or landing tab) is used to house your raw data. This raw data is expected to be updated regularly. It is important to note that when data is updated in this tab, column order/ structure and column names should remain static and should not be changed. The structure within this tab should not be altered in any way and will be used to feed into the next tab, the *staging tab*.

The **staging** tab is used to reference data from within the *input* tab, so that any additions/modifications to the data can be made without permanently altering the raw data. Essentially, the staging tab often mimics the structure of your raw data tab, while adding new columns, measures, formulas, VLOOKUPs from other spreadsheets, etc. Think of this tab as the place where your data is prepared and enhanced so that it contains all of the required data needed to create your reports and graphs.

The **report** tab is used to create your final reports (i.e. metrics, graphs, summaries, etc.) that will be used by or distributed to end users. All of the data that is used in this tab is taken from the *staging* tab. This tab should contain little or no data formatting or restructuring, and should focus primarily on reporting.

There are a few benefits to organizing your Excel files this way. First, it is much easier to keep your data organized when your raw data has a dedicated landing tab. Second, you can easily audit your data for errors and know where they are coming from. This is made easier since your input tab will not contain any data modifications. You will be able to tell if your imported data is incorrect (*input* tab) or if there is an error within your formulas (*staging* tab). Third, when new data is added or changed in the *input* tab, all of the updated data will automatically flow to the *staging* tab, and into the *report* tab (assuming you have set up your references correctly). No manual effort is required. Lastly, you can hide and protect your *input* and *staging* tabs before you share your Excel file with others. This way, users will only see the output results (the *report* tab) and cannot make any changes to the raw data or your data modifications.

PRINCIPLE #17: DO NOT CORRECT OTHER PEOPLE'S MISTAKES

This principle is important when standardizing a process that relies on other people's data inputs. When creating a standardized or automated process, you will need to analyze and understand all of your data sources that feed into the process. If the process relies on data inputs from others, and they are entering or organizing the data incorrectly, do *not* correct the mistakes yourself. You should alert the individual(s) responsible as to the errors and ask that they correct them. This also applies to processes that are already established and have incorrect data being fed into them. Always go back to the owner of the data source and have them make the corrections. Never do it yourself.

You may be asked (or pressured) to fix the mistakes yourself in the meantime as an attempt to "save time" so that your work can continue. While correcting other people's mistakes will save time in the short-term, it also ensures that inefficiency within the organization continues in the long-term. People are creatures of habit, and if you start fixing their mistakes, they will get used to you doing it for them.

When the owner of the data source corrects their own mistakes, it gives them the opportunity to understand and recognize the issues, prevent them from occurring next time, and encourages a permanent resolution in the long-term. If you correct the data mistakes for them, you have ultimately shifted the onus of responsibility onto yourself. You are also ensuring that the errors continue to happen and that no permanent resolution will occur. If this occurs, your standardized process will contain incorrect data on a regular basis, causing users to lose trust in your data, and discouraging them from using your reports.

PRINCIPLE #18: DON'T PRETEND TO BE A DOMAIN EXPERT

There will be times when your reports require data from other business areas outside your domain of expertise. You may be in IT and require customer mapping data from Sales, or you may be in Sales and require forecasting information from Supply Chain. When this occurs, you should always get the required data from the appropriate business area expert, and not try to recreate the data yourself.

For example, if you are in IT and require customer mapping data, do not attempt to map the customer hierarchies yourself if you lack the required business knowledge. This may seem like an obvious thing to avoid, but it is easy to fall into. Deadlines may be creeping up and you may have reached out to the data owners numerous times with no success. So, to keep things moving, you decide to "take a stab at it" yourself.

You might also be tempted to extract data from a sales portal you have never used before. Yes, you can try to pull the data yourself and hope that you pulled it correctly, or you can ask someone who has used the portal and understands the data for assistance. In case you are wondering, the latter option is the correct one!

Datasets are not always what they seem and may contain

nuances that only those who work with the data on a regular basis understand and recognize. For example, column names may be labelled incorrectly and contain different values (e.g. a column named "Product Category" may actually contain product names), or values may not always represent what you think they do (e.g. are currency values in USD, GBP, CAD?). There is no way for you to recognize these nuances if you are not familiar with the dataset. As a result, it is best you ask an expert in that domain to assist you or provide you with the data directly.

Recreating datasets yourself is never optimal if you lack the data knowledge. This usually results in wasted time and required re-work, as it is highly unlikely for someone unfamiliar with a particular dataset to recreate the data correctly the first time. If you still think you can proceed, I need to ask: how lucky do you think you are?

PRINCIPLE #19:
ENSURE COMMITMENT
FROM DATA OWNERS

If your standardized process requires data inputs from multiple data owners, it is important that you establish who those data owners are early on, and determine whether they can provide you the dataset you need (in the format you need) on a regular basis.

If you plan to create an ad-hoc report that will only be used once, and will never be updated again, then you can ignore this principle. If you are creating a standardized process that will be used on an ongoing basis, you will need to ensure all of your data sources' owners are identified, that they understand the data format you need, and that they are able to provide you with the data on a regular basis.

If your process requires data inputs from other individuals on a regular basis, but they are not able to provide you with data regularly, you should reconsider your process. You will either need to convince the data owner to send you the data regularly, or find another method for getting your data (preferably from an automatic source). There is nothing more wasteful and disheartening than creating the most informative, most enlightening, and most beautiful report that will only be used *once*.

Data sources and their owners should be established early and should not be changed or altered, if possible. Changes to your data source may lead to a change in data owners, which will lead to changes in the data's format, which will ultimately result in technical modifications to your report. Changing data owners, while is sometimes unavoidable, will have a domino effect that will impact your entire process. You will need to ensure that the new data owner is familiar with your process and is committed to providing you with the data you need. So be sure to choose your data sources and owners wisely the first time.

PRINCIPLE #20: LIMIT THE NUMBER OF MAPPING FILES

When you have several data sources that do not share common columns or values, you will require the use of one or more mapping files. These mapping files will allow you to associate data between tables that would not otherwise be possible.

For example, suppose you receive sales data on your organization's products from a customer. Internally, you most likely have an identifier for all of your products. However, your customers likely use different product identifiers of their own.

The figures below provide an example. *Figure 20.1.1* shows a simple example of a table containing product identifiers and product names within an organization, *Figure 20.1.2* shows a simple example of an external table containing sales data for your organization's products from a customer, and *Figure 20.1.3* shows an example of a mapping file that would be used to associate your organization's product numbers to your customer's product numbers from the sales table.

Internal Table	
Product #	Product Name
1234	Prod. 1
2345	Prod. 2
3456	Prod. 3
4567	Prod. 4
5678	Prod. 5
6789	Prod. 6
7890	Prod. 7
8901	Prod. 8
9012	Prod. 9

Figure 20.1.1: Example of an internal product table

Customer Data		
Product #	Product Name	Sales $
852	Prod. 114	100
963	Prod. 226	60
741	Prod. 689	150
123	Prod. 125	20
456	Prod. 458	200
654	Prod. 689	10
753	Prod. 701	50
357	Prod. 812	100
1530	Prod. 955	70

Figure 20.1.2: Example of an external customer table

Mapping Table		
Internal Product #	Customer Product #	Product Name
1234	852	Prod. 1
2345	963	Prod. 2
3456	741	Prod. 3
4567	123	Prod. 4
5678	456	Prod. 5
6789	654	Prod. 6
7890	753	Prod. 7
8901	357	Prod. 8
9012	1530	Prod. 9

Figure 20.1.3: Example of a mapping table

Using the mapping file in *Figure 20.1.3* allows you to link your internal product table (*Figure 20.1.1*) to your customer's external sales table (*Figure 20.1.2*). Mapping files tend to be a necessity to reporting since data is rarely perfect and hardly ever aligns to other datasets.

While mapping files are helpful in making associations in your data that otherwise would not exist, they can also backfire and cause complexity in your processes. They require constant maintenance, and increased work time. This is likely if your report contains several datasets that need to be linked, requiring the use of several mapping files.

Imagine having to maintain five or six mapping files every month, some with hundreds of rows, and the extra time needed to ensure all files are up-to-date. If not, the data in your reports would be outdated and contain unassigned values. The beauty of a standardized (and hopefully automated) process is that it reduces or eliminates the manual effort needed for it to run. If you add the maintenance of several mapping files to the equation, the time saved implementing the standardized process will be spent maintaining the mapping files.

While more mapping files will increase your ability to associate different datasets that do not share commonalities, they will also increase the maintenance time needed to ensure your reports are accurate. This tends to create a paradox, since if you are spending most of your time maintaining mapping files, then you will have less time to discover insights. However, insights are more likely when you associate different datasets, requiring multiple mapping files. Maintaining this balance between datasets that do not share commonalities and mapping files will be up to you and the objectives of your report(s). The only way to reduce the number of mapping files is to ensure your datasets can be linked with common fields (such as keys), or to exclude them altogether from your reports. So balance carefully!

CONCLUSION

I hope this book has inspired you to apply these principles in your work to organize your data and implement standardized reporting processes that will allow you to create clean, standardized, and more efficient spreadsheets and reports.

The principles mentioned here are intended to give you a foundation upon which to build. Once you start implementing them in your day-to-day tasks, I am certain that you will look at data differently, and begin to discover other data organization and standardization best practices.

As I mentioned at the beginning, my goal for this book is to help rid the world of terrible spreadsheets that prevent us from properly analyzing data, waste our time, and get in the way of progress. I hope that now you also feel the same way, and that I've gained one more ally in this long and painful fight. I look forward to fighting this great battle with you, one terrible spreadsheet at a time.

ABOUT THE AUTHOR

Anthony Barbieri is a certified business analytics professional working for an international consumer packaged goods company. His goal is to rid the world of data and process inefficiencies, and bridge the gap between business and technology.